SACRED

ATB unaccompanied

OXFORD

T0346277

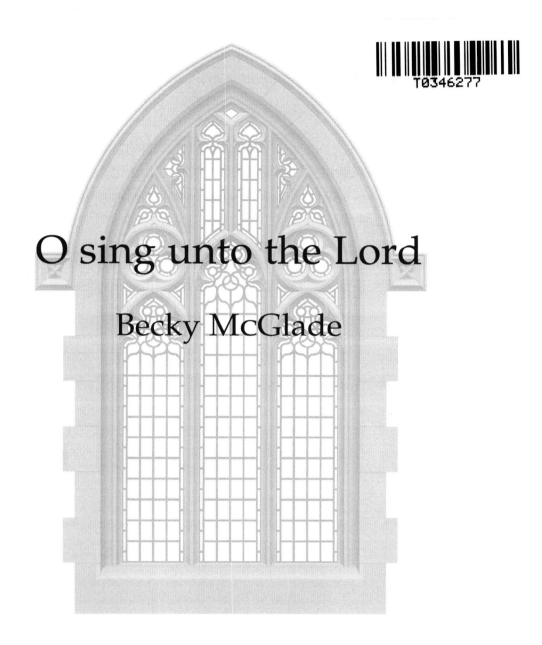

O sing unto the Lord

Becky McGlade

MUSIC DEPARTMENT

OXFORD

UNIVERSITY PRESS

for the choir of York Minster in celebration of the
return to choral services after the initial pandemic lockdown

O sing unto the Lord

Psalm 98:1

BECKY McGLADE

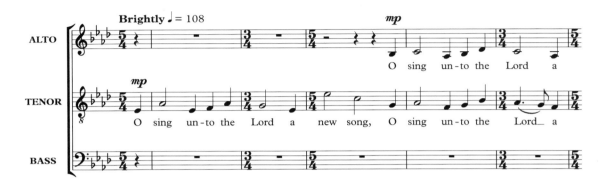

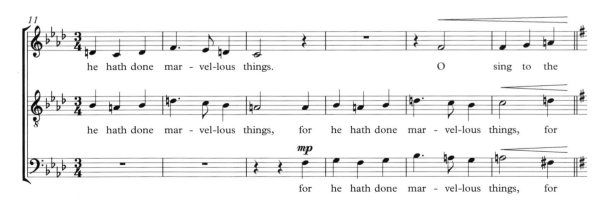

First performed by the Choir of York Minster, directed by Robert Sharpe, at York Minster on 9 September 2020.   Duration: 2.5 mins

Printed in Great Britain

OXFORD UNIVERSITY PRESS, MUSIC DEPARTMENT, GREAT CLARENDON STREET, OXFORD OX2 6DP

X813 O sing unto the Lord McGLADE

ISBN 978-0-19-355106-0

9 780193 551060